Carolyn's Lit. Guide

Adventures

3-4 Grade

By Carolyn Oravitz

Fun, Fantastic, Fantabulous Books to Read and Enjoy!

<u>LITERATURE GUIDES</u>

With Chapter Questions and End of the Book

ISBN: **0997197226**
ISBN-13: **978-0997197228**

ACKNOWLEDGEMENTS

Mr. Popper's Penguins by Richard and Florence Atwater, Little Brown and Company

Stolen! A Pony Called Pebbles by Wendy Orr, Henry Holt & Company

Charlotte's Web by E. B. White, Scholastic

I Survived the Sinking of the Titanic, 1912, I Survived Series, by Lauren Tarshis, Scholastic

The Knight at Dawn Magic Tree House #2, by Mary Pope Osborne, Random House

I Survived the Battle of Gettysburg, 1863, I Survived Series, by Lauren Tarshis, Scholastic

Parent/Teacher Information

Carolyn's Lit. Guide Adventures

List of benefits:

These literature guides have been designed as supplemental materials to aid the student in building reading skills.

The grade level books have been carefully selected and have been proven to be of great interest to students, helping motivate the most reluctant reader as well as those children who enjoy and excel at reading. Some of these books are abridged or adapted versions of classics that introduce students to timeless themes, plots, and characters. These versions help the child develop a love for reading while improving his or her reading skills. Children may choose to read the unabridged version of the same book after reading the abridged one.

Each fun, yet educational, set of books contain multiple-choice chapter questions to work on while reading. Each set also has an and end of the book open-book test with 25 multiple-choice questions to take after the book has been carefully read and the chapter questions have been checked, corrected, and studied.

Easy to follow independent work and students will only need assistance when the questions and tests have been completed. Parent/teacher answers are provided with chapter numbers to follow up.

Book sets come in Grades 3 and 4, Grades 5 and 6, and Grades 7 and 8.

Books can be found on Amazon and other websites where books are sold.

Student Instructions: Read these fun, fantastic, fantabulous books from the list above and then answer the chapter questions. After you have carefully read each book and have had your chapter question answers checked, take the end of the book test. Then have your teacher or parent check your answers.

Contents

LITERATURE GUIDE ONE

Mr. Popper's Penguins

By Richard and Florence Atwater

Chapter Questions

Student Instructions: Read the book and answer the questions as you finish each chapter. If you need help, you may look in the book for help.

1. What was Mr. Popper's job? _____ (Chapter 1)

    A. plumber

    B. electrician

    C. house painter

2. Mr. Popper liked to read about what region in the world? _____ (Chapter 2)

    A. South America

    B. South Pole

    C. South Dakota

3. Who sent Mr. Popper a surprise package? _____ (Chapter 3)

    A. Admiral Drake

    B. Mrs. Popper

    C. Santa Claus

4. What did the penguin, Captain Cook, eat? _____ (Chapter 4)

    A. gumdrops

    B. grapes

    C. goldfish

5. Mr. Popper had the serviceman put holes in their icebox refrigerator. What else did he want done to the icebox? _____ (Chapter 5)

    A. Mr. Popper wanted the serviceman to put a radio in the icebox.

    B. Mr. Popper wanted the serviceman to put a handle on the inside of the icebox door.

    C. Mr. Popper wanted the serviceman to add a back door to the icebox.

6. Why did the policeman come to the Popper's house? _____ (Chapter 6)

    A.   The serviceman said Mr. Popper didn't pay him.

    B.   The serviceman said Mr. Popper had a strange animal in his house.

    C. The serviceman thought Mr. Popper stole his tools.

7. Why was Captain Cook collecting things from around the house? _____
(Chapter 7)

   A. He wanted to help clean the house.

   B. He wanted to impress people.

   C. He wanted to build a nest.

8. Why did the newspaper man want to take a picture of Captain Cook? _____
(Chapter 8)

   A. He had never seen a penguin on a leash.

   B. He had never seen a penguin in the town.

   C. Both A and B

9. When Mr. Popper returned home from the barber shop, Mrs. Popper was surprised that he no longer looked neat, like he did when he went out. How did he get messed up? _____ (Chapter 9)

   A. He slid down three flights of steps on his stomach.

   B. He was painting and got paint on his clothes.

   C. He got messed up from cleaning the barber shop.

10. Why wasn't Captain Cook happy anymore? _____ (Chapter 10)

   A. He was lonely.

   B. He was hungry.

   C. He was sick.

11. Why was Captain Cook happy again? _____ (Chapter 11)

   A. Greta, a female penguin, came to live with him.

   B. Mr. Popper sent Captain Cook back to the South Pole.

   C. He ate a lot of shrimp.

12. How many baby penguins hatched from the eggs? _____ (Chapter 12)

   A. six

   B. eight

   C. ten

13. What idea did Mr. Popper get as a way to earn more money? _____
(Chapter 13)

   A. He wanted to have a trained penguins act.

   B. He wanted to paint pictures of penguins.

   C. He wanted to have the children do a circus act.

14. Why did Mr. Popper take all the penguins on a bus? _____ (Chapter 14)

   A. to show Mr. Greenbaum their penguin act

   B. to show the penguins to the driver and passengers

   C. to take the penguins to the pond to go swimming

15. How did Mr. Greenbaum and the audience like the Popper's Performing
    Penguins act? _____ (Chapter 15)

   A. They didn't like it at all.

   B. They fell asleep because it was boring.

   C. They cheered and clapped.

16. The penguins interfered with other acts, but the audience did this. _____
(Chapter 16)

   A. The audience shouted and ordered them off the stage.

   B. The audience liked the act better than ever.

   C. The audience got up and left the show in protest.

17. Popper's Performing Penguins became famous, and people stood in line to
    see them. How long was the line? _____ (Chapter 17)

   A. twenty feet

   B. twenty yards

   C. a half mile

18. Why did the manager of the Regal Theater want to have Mr. Popper
    arrested? _____ (Chapter 18)

   A. The manager said the penguins threw the place into a panic.

   B. The manager said they were in the wrong theater.

   C. Both A and B

19. What choices was Mr. Popper given in chapter nineteen? _____
   (Chapter 19)

   A. He and the penguins could be in the movies or move to the North Pole.

   B. He and the penguins could be in the movies or move to the South Pole.

   C. He and the penguins could go to the North Pole or the South Pole.

20. What was the final decision regarding the future of Mr. Popper and his penguins? _____ (Chapter 20)

   A. Mr. Popper and his penguins would make movies together.

   B. Mr. Popper and his penguins would go to the North Pole.

   C. Mr. Popper and his penguins would go to the South Pole.

Student, when you've checked and corrected all your answers in this literature guide, and you've read every page in the book, then take the End of the Book Test.

You can find the answers to these questions on page 84.

Mr. Popper's Penguins

By Richard and Florence Atwater

End of the Book Test

Student Instructions: Student, each question is worth 4 points. Let's see how well you've read this exciting book. You may use this as an open book test and complete it within a 30-minute time limit. After you take the test, have your teacher/parent score the test for you. Then correct the wrong answers by reviewing the book for the correct answers.

1. What was Mr. Popper's job? _____ (Chapter 1)

    A. plumber

    B. electrician

    C. house painter

2. The setting of a story tells the time and place a story happens. What is the setting at the beginning of this story? _____ (Chapter 1)

    A. September in the city of Stillwater

    B. October in the city of Jallen

    C. November in the town of Sullivan

3. Why was Mr. Popper always so absent-minded? _____ (Chapter 1)

    A. He was always dreaming about decorating big houses.

    B. He was always dreaming about far-away countries.

    C. He was always dreaming about going on American Idol.

4. How do we know that Mr. Popper was interested in the Poles? _____ (Chapter 1)

    A. He often sat through three shows of Polar movies.

    B. He always got out new books about the Arctic or Antarctica at the library.

    C. Both A and B

5. Mr. and Mrs. Popper were listening to the radio and heard Admiral Drake say hello to Mr. Popper. Why did this famous Arctic explorer, Admiral Drake, talk to Mr. Popper? _____ (Chapter 2)

    A. Mrs. Popper had written a letter about her husband to Admiral Drake.

    B. Mr. Popper had written a letter to Admiral Drake about penguins.

    C. Mr. Popper's kids had written to Admiral Drake about penguins.

6. Who sent Mr. Popper a surprise package? _____ (Chapter 3)

   A. Admiral Drake

   B. Mrs. Popper

   C. Santa Claus

7. Mr. Popper and his family thought the package contained something alive. What were some clues leading them to this conclusion? _____ (Chapter 3)

   A. The box was marked "Unpack at once."

   B. The box had air holes, and was marked "Keep cool."

   C. Both A and B

8. What was the size of the first penguin? _____ (Chapter 3)

   A. 2 ½ yards

   B. 2 ½ feet

   C. 3 ½ feet

9. What did the penguin, Captain Cook, eat? _____ (Chapter 4)

   A. gumdrops

   B. grapes

   C. goldfish

10. Mr. Popper had the serviceman put holes in their icebox refrigerator. What else did he want done to the icebox? _____ (Chapter 5)

    A. Mr. Popper wanted the serviceman to put a radio in the icebox.

    B. Mr. Popper wanted the serviceman to put a handle on the inside of the icebox door.

    C. Mr. Popper wanted the serviceman to add a back door to the icebox.

11. Why did the policeman come to Mr. Popper's house? _____ (Chapter 6)

   A. The serviceman said Mr. Popper didn't pay him.

   B. The serviceman said Mr. Popper had a strange animal in his house.

   C. The serviceman thought Mr. Popper stole his tools.

12. Why was Captain Cook collecting things from around the house? _____
   (Chapter 7)

   A. He wanted to help clean the house.

   B. He wanted to impress people.

   C. He wanted to build a nest.

13. Why did the newspaper man want to take a picture of Captain Cook? _____
   (Chapter 8)

   A. He had never seen a penguin on a leash.

   B. He had never seen a penguin in their town.

   C. Both A and B

14. What did the barber say to get the penguin out of the barber shop? _____
   (Chapter 9)

   A. This is no circus.

   B. This is no zoo.

   C. This is no South Pole.

15. When Mr. Popper returned home from the barber shop, Mrs. Popper was
   surprised that he no longer looked neat like he did when he went out. How did
   he get messed up? _____ (Chapter 9)

   A. He slid down three flights of steps on his stomach.

   B. He was painting and got paint on his clothes.

   C. He got dirty from cleaning the barber shop.

16. Why wasn't Captain Cook happy anymore? _____ (Chapter 10)

   A. He was lonely.

   B. He was hungry.

   C. He was sick.

17. Why was Captain Cook happy again? _____ (Chapter 11)

   A. Greta, a female penguin, came to live with him.

   B. Mr. Popper sent Captain Cook back to the South Pole.

18. How many baby penguins hatched from the eggs? _____ (Chapter 12)

   A. six

   B. eight

   C. ten

19. What idea did Mr. Popper get as a way to earn more money? _____
(Chapter 13)

   A. He wanted to have a trained penguins act.

   B. He wanted to paint pictures of penguins.

   C. He wanted to have the children do a circus act.

20. Why did Mr. Popper take all the penguins on a bus? _____ (Chapter 14)

   A. to show Mr. Greenbaum their penguin act

   B. to show the penguins to the driver and passengers

   C. to take the penguins to the pond to go swimming

21. The penguins interfered with other acts, but the audience did this. _____
(Chapter 16)

   A. The audience shouted and ordered them off the stage.

   B. The audience liked the act better than ever.

   C. The audience got up and left the show in protest.

22. Popper's Performing Penguins became famous and people stood in line to see them. How long was the line? _____ (Chapter 17)

    A. twenty feet

    B. twenty yards

    C. a half mile

23. Why did the manager of the Regal Theater want to have Mr. Popper arrested? _____ (Chapter 18)

    A. The manager said the penguins threw the place into a panic.

    B. The manager said they were in the wrong theater.

    C. Both A and B

24. What choices was Mr. Popper given in this chapter? _____ (Chapter 19)

    A. He and the penguins could be in the movies, or move to the North Pole.

    B. He and the penguins could be in the movies, or move to the South Pole.

    C. He and the penguins could go to the North Pole or the South Pole.

25. What was the final decision regarding the future of Mr. Popper and his penguins? _____ (Chapter 20)

    A. Mr. Popper and his penguins would make movies together.

    B. Mr. Popper and his penguins would go to the North Pole.

    C. Mr. Popper and his penguins would go to the South Pole.

You can find the answers to these questions on page 85.

LITERATURE GUIDE TWO

Stolen! A Pony Called Pebbles

By Wendy Orr

Chapter Questions

Student Instructions: Read the book and answer the questions as you finish each chapter. If you need help, you may look in the book for help.

1. What happened in chapter one? _____ (Chapter 1)

    A. Two thieves stole two horses.

    B. Two thieves stole one horse.

    C. One thief stole two horses.

2. In chapter two, we meet a girl who loved horses. She read about them, drew pictures of them, and even pretended to run like one. What was this girl's name? _____ (Chapter 2)

    A. Hannah

    B. Amy

    C. Pebbles

3. What did the thieves do with the horses? _____ (Chapter 3)

    A. The thieves hid them in a big barn.

    B. The thieves hid them at a circus with circus horses.

    C. The thieves hid them in the park.

4. Why did the thieves want to make the black stallion look white? _____ (Chapter 4)

    A. Everyone was looking for a stolen black horse.

    B. Everyone likes white horses best.

    C. Everyone would think that Midnight was Pebbles.

5. Amy went for a walk in the park with Hannah's family. When they were walking, Amy thought she could hear this. _____ (Chapter 5)

    A. a waterfall

    B. a horse

    C. a cow

6. What did Amy do for Pebbles? _____ (Chapter 6)

    A. She rode Pebbles around the park.

    B. She rode Pebbles out on the road.

C. She rescued Pebbles when she was caught in the fence.

7. What did Amy feed the horse when it was hungry? _____ (Chapter 7)

   A. carrots and grass

   B. hamburgers and French fries

   C. candy and Coke

8. Where did they take the horse? _____ (Chapter 8)

   A. to the fenced-in area of the park

   B. to the Rainbow Street Animal Shelter

   C. to the Rainbow Race Track

9. When Amy went to the shelter to see Silvie, Mona let her do this. _____ (Chapter 9)

   A. Mona let Amy race the horse.

   B. Mona let Amy bathe the horse.

   C. Mona let Amy brush the horse.

10. Amy was calling the horse Silvie. Then she found out this was the real name of the horse they found. _____ (Chapter 10)

    A. Midnight

    B. Pebbles

    C. Silver

11. What was Amy's reward for saving Pebbles? _____ (Chapter 11)

    A. Amy was allowed to ride Pebbles on Sundays.

    B. Amy got Pebbles' son for her very own.

    C. Both A and B

Student, when you've checked and corrected all your answers in this literature guide and you've read every page in the book, then take the End of the Book Test.

You can find the answers to these questions on page 86.

Stolen! A Pony Called Pebbles

By Wendy Orr

End of the Book Test

<u>Student Instructions</u>: Student, each question is worth 4 points. Let's see how well you've read this exciting book. You may use this as an open book test and complete it within a 30-minute time limit. After you take the test, have your teacher/parent score the test for you. Then correct the wrong answers by reviewing the book for the correct answers.

1. Why did two men take two horses in chapter one? _____ (Chapter 1)

    A. Two thieves stole the horses to sell them and get a lot of money.

    B. Two thieves stole the horses so they could ride them in a circus.

    C. Two thieves stole the horses to give them to their daughters.

2. In chapter one, we read about a famous race horse. What was his name? _____ (Chapter 1)

    A. Daystar

    B. Afternoon Magic

    C. Midnight

3. When the thieves stole the big black racehorse, they also took the smaller white one. Why did they take the small white one too? _____ (Chapter 1)

    A. The thieves each wanted their own horse.

    B. The big horse would not go anywhere without the small white one.

    C. The thieves liked white horses better than black ones.

4. Why did Amy's mother say they couldn't have a horse? _____ (Chapter 2)

    A. Horses were too mean.

    B. Horses were too lazy.

    C. Horses were too expensive.

5. Amy's dad called Amy and her friend Hannah twins, even though they didn't look alike. What was the same about them? _____ (Chapter 2)

    A. They both had black hair.

    B. They both loved animals.

    C. They both loved cats.

6. In chapter two, we read that the horses whinnied as they bumped around in the horse trailer. What does whinny mean? _____ (Chapter 2)

   A. Whinny is a noise horses make.

   B. Whinny is when horses stomp their feet.

   C. Whinny is when horses sleep.

7. What did the thieves do with the horses? _____ (Chapter 3)

   A. The thieves hid them on a farm and put a fence around them.

   B. The thieves hid them at a circus with circus horses.

   C. The thieves hid them in the park and put a fence around them.

8. Why did Midnight want to be near Pebbles? _____ (Chapter 3)

   A. Pebbles made Midnight feel calmer.

   B. Pebbles showed Midnight where food was.

   C. Pebbles could run faster than Midnight.

9. Why did Hannah go to the Rainbow Street Shelter on Saturdays? _____ (Chapter 4)

   A. to help Mona and Juan and the dogs

   B. to help the horses

   C. to earn some spending money

10. Why did the thieves want to make the black stallion look white? _____ (Chapter 4)

   A. Everyone was looking for a stolen black horse.

   B. Everyone liked white horses best.

   C. Everyone would think that Midnight was Pebbles.

11. Who was Peanut? _____ (Chapter 5)

   A. Hannah's horse

   B. Hannah's dog

   C. Hannah's brother

12. Amy went for a walk in the park with Hannah's family. When they were walking, Amy thought she could hear this. _____ (Chapter 5)

   A. a waterfall

   B. a horse

   C. a cow

13. Who walked with Amy and Hannah's family in the park? _____ (Chapter 5)

   A. Amy's dog

   B. Hannah's dog

14. What happened to the two thieves? _____ (Chapter 5)

   A. They escaped and were never caught.

   B. The policemen caught them.

15. Why did Pebbles get stuck in the wire fence? _____ (Chapter 6)

   A. She was trying to do a trick.

   B. She was trying to jump over the fence to escape.

   C. She was trying to get some fresh, green food from a tree.

16. What did Amy do for Pebbles? _____ (Chapter 6)

   A. She rode Pebbles around the park.

   B. She rode Pebbles out on the road.

   C. She rescued Pebbles when she was caught in the fence.

17. Amy didn't know the white horse's name was Pebbles, so she called her this name. _____ (Chapter 7)

   A. Stormy

   B. Silvie

   C. Sleepy

18. What did Amy feed the horse when it was hungry? _____ (Chapter 7)

    A. carrots and grass

    B. bananas and apples

    C. bread and butter

19. Where did they take the horse? _____ (Chapter 8)

    A. to the fenced-in area of the park

    B. to the Rainbow Street Animal Shelter

    C. to the Rainbow Race Track

20. What reward would Amy like for finding Pebbles? _____ (Chapter 8)

    A. to be able to ride Pebbles

    B. to be given 100 dollars

    C. to get a new puppy

21. When Amy went to the shelter to see Silvie, Mona let her do this. _____ (Chapter 9)

    A. Mona let Amy race the horse.

    B. Mona let Amy bathe the horse.

    C. Mona let Amy brush the horse.

22. Did Pebbles like to be brushed? _____ (Chapter 9)

    A. yes

    B. no

23. In chapter ten, why did Amy want to cry? _____ (Chapter 10)

    A. She didn't want to go back to school after vacation.

    B. She thought she'd never see Silvie again.

    C. She decided that she no longer liked horses.

24. What was Amy's reward for saving Pebbles? _____ (Chapter 11)

    A. Amy was allowed to ride Pebbles on Sundays.

    B. Amy got Pebbles' son for her very own.

    C. Both A and B

25. What was Pebbles' son's name? _____ (Chapter 11)

    A. Silver Pebbles

    B. Silver Shadow

    C. Silver Colt

You can find the answers to these questions on page 87.

LITERATURE GUIDE THREE

Charlotte's Web

By E. B. White

Chapter Questions

Student Instructions: Read the book and answer the questions as you finish each chapter. If you need help, you may look in the book for help.

1. Why did Mr. Avery plan to kill a pig? _____ (Chapter 1)

   A. The pig was too small.

   B. The pig would be too much trouble.

   C. Both A and B

2. How much did they sell Wilbur for? _____ (Chapter 2)

   A. 6 dollars

   B. 16 dollars

   C. 26 dollars

3. What did Wilbur conclude after his exciting day of escaping from the barn? _____ (Chapter 3)

   A. He was too young to go out into the world alone.

   B. Being penned up in his own yard was better than freedom.

   C. Both A and B

4. Wilbur thought he couldn't endure loneliness anymore, but then this happened. _____ (Chapter 4)

   A. He made friends with a rat.

   B. He heard a small voice say, "I'll be your friend."

   C. He decided he didn't really need friends.

5. Charlotte looked at Wilbur and said, "Salutations." What are salutations? _____ (Chapter 5)

   A. a way of greeting

   B. a way of saluting

   C. a way of saying be quiet

6. Charlotte said, "If that ancient egg ever breaks, this barn will be untenable."
   What did she mean by that? _____ (Chapter 6)

   A. They would not be able to live there because of the smell.

   B. They would be able to eat eggs for breakfast.

   C. The egg might hatch into a cute little duckling.

7. What bad news did Wilbur hear in chapter seven? _____ (Chapter 7)

   A. He was going to die.

   B. Charlotte was going to die.

   C. Fern was going to die.

8. In chapter eight Fern's mother, Mrs. Arable, found this out about Fern. _____
   (Chapter 8)

   A. Fern could hear the animals talking.

   B. Fern wanted more pigs for pets.

   C. Fern wanted to go to a doctor.

9. What impossible task did Wilbur attempt in chapter nine? _____ (Chapter 9)

   A. He tried to spin a web.

   B. He tried to lay an egg.

   C. He tried to escape to the forest again.

10. What exploded in chapter ten? _____ (Chapter 10)

    A. a small bomb

    B. Templeton's rotten egg

    C. some fireworks

11. What miracle occurred in chapter eleven? _____ (Chapter 11)

    A. Wilbur learned to spin a web.

    B. Charlotte wrote words in her web.

    C. Dew glistened in the early morning light.

12. Why did Charlotte call a meeting for all the animals in the barn cellar? _____ (Chapter 12)

    A. to get new ideas for a slogan to spin in Charlotte's web

    B. to help save Wilbur's life

    C. both A and B

13. What was Templeton looking for in the dump? _____ (Chapter 13)

    A. another rotten egg to hide

    B. another word for Charlotte to spin in her web

    C. another rat to have for a friend

14. How did Dr. Dorian respond to Mrs. Arable's concern that Fern thought animals can talk? _____ (Chapter 14)

    A. He said Fern was only pretending.

    B. He said Fern needed medication.

    C. He said he was ready to believe Fern.

15. Charlotte said she was versatile. What does versatile mean? _____ (Chapter 15)

    A. being able to recite verses of a poem

    B. being able to turn with ease from one thing to another

    C. being full of eggs

16. Why did Wilbur faint in chapter sixteen? _____ (Chapter 16)

    A. He was nervous about going to the fair.

    B. He heard Mr. Arable say they'd get good ham and bacon from him.

    C. He saw Templeton and was afraid of rats.

17. Why didn't Charlotte like the pig named Uncle? _____ (Chapter 17)

   A. He was too noisy.

   B. He cracked weak jokes.

   C. Both A and B

18. Charlotte wove the word HUMBLE into her web. What did she say humble meant? _____ (Chapter 18)

   A. not proud and near the ground

   B. not proud and not large

   C. not large and near the ground

19. What was Charlotte's magnum opus? _____ (Chapter 19)

   A. her great work

   B. her egg sac

   C. both A and B

20. Who came to the rescue when Wilbur fainted? _____ (Chapter 20)

   A. Templeton bit his tail and revived him.

   B. Avery threw water on him and revived him.

   C. Charlotte called to him, and he woke up.

21. Why did Templeton finally agree to take Charlotte's egg sac? _____ (Chapter 21)

   A. Wilbur agreed to give him his prize blue ribbon.

   B. Wilbur would let Templeton eat first when Lurvy brought his food.

   C. Wilbur begged him, and Templeton agreed because he was a nice rat.

22. Charlotte's death was sad, but Wilbur was happy because she left him with this. _____ (Chapter 22)

   A. three special webs

   B. three of her children

   C. three blue ribbons

Student, when you've checked and corrected all your answers in this literature guide and you've read every page in the book, then take the End of the Book Test.

You can find the answers to these questions on page 88.

Charlotte's Web

By E. B. White

End of the Book Test

<u>Student Instructions:</u> Student, each question is worth 4 points. Let's see how well you've read this exciting book. You may use this as an open book test and complete it within a 30-minute time limit. After you take the test, have your teacher/parent score the test for you. Then correct the wrong answers by reviewing the book for the correct answers.

1. Fern wanted to "rid the world of injustice." What did she think was unjust? _____ (Chapter 1)

    A. killing cows for food

    B. killing a pig because he was small

    C. killing squirrels with an air rifle

2. What lesson was Mr. Arable trying to teach Avery when Avery asked if he could have a pig too? _____ (Chapter 1)

    A. to get up earlier

    B. to not use a wooden dagger

    C. to help his sister

3. Why couldn't Wilbur follow the instructions his friends were giving him? _____ (Chapter 3)

    A. They were all telling him to do different things.

    B. They were all telling him to go uphill.

    C. They were all telling him to go downhill.

4. After a dark rainy day, Lurvy dumped the slops for Wilbur to eat, but Wilbur didn't want the food. What did he want? _____ (Chapter 4)

    A. Wilbur wanted love.

    B. Wilbur wanted a friend.

    C. Both A and B

5. Why wouldn't Templeton be Wilbur's friend when Wilbur asked him to play with him? _____ (Chapter 4)

    A. Templeton didn't like pigs.

    B. Templeton spent most of his time sleeping or eating.

    C. Templeton had to take care of his family.

6. What saved Wilbur when he thought he couldn't endure the awful loneliness anymore? _____ (Chapter 4)

A. a small voice that sounded like another pig

B. a small voice that sounded rather thin but pleasant

C. a small voice of one of the geese

7. Wilbur was anxious to meet his new friend, Charlotte, but something about her made him sad. What made him sad? _____ (Chapter 5)

A. His new friend was bloodthirsty.

B. His new friend was lazy.

C. His new friend was too busy for him.

8. Wilbur thought Charlotte was fierce, brutal, and scheming, but he liked two things about her. What were they? _____ (Chapter 5)

A. She was pretty and clever.

B. She was small and quiet.

C. She was small and cruel.

9. How was Templeton, the rat, described? _____ (Chapter 6)

A. He had no morals and no conscience.

B. He had no scruples and no milk of rodent kindness.

C. Both A and B

10. The old sheep described the plans to kill young pigs as this. _____
(Chapter 7)

A. a regular congestion

B. a regular conscience

C. a regular conspiracy

11. Why was Mrs. Arable worried about Fern in chapter eight? _____ (Chapter 8)

   A. Fern said the animals talked.

   B. Fern spent too much time at the barn cellar.

   C. Both A and B

12. Charlotte said she was glad to be a sedentary spider. What does sedentary mean? _____ (Chapter 9)

   A. staying still in one place

   B. many-legged with spinnerets

   C. filled with sand or sediment

13. Charlotte said people are very gullible. How did she think she could fool people? _____ (Chapter 10)

   A. She could trick them into thinking Wilbur would not make good bacon.

   B. She could trick them by weaving a word in her web.

   C. She could trick them into forgetting to feed Wilbur.

14. What saved Charlotte's life in chapter ten? _____ (Chapter 10)

   A. Templeton's rotten egg

   B. Wilbur's rotten egg

   C. Fern's rotten egg

15. What was the mysterious sign that happened on the farm? _____ (Chapter 11)

   A. Wilbur continued to grow larger.

   B. The words SOME PIG were woven into a spider web.

   C. Wilbur was no longer ignoring his food.

16. What explanation did the minister give for the words on the spider web? He said the words proved this. _____ (Chapter 11)

    A. Humans must realize spiders are intelligent beings.

    B. Humans must accept that pigs are special animals.

    C. Humans must be on the watch for the coming of wonders.

17. What words proved Templeton's true character and feelings about Wilbur? _____ (Chapter 12)

    A. Templeton said, "Let him die."

    B. Templeton said, "I'd help him if I could."

    C. Templeton said, "I'm only a rat, and I'm too little."

18. How did Fern's mother react when Fern repeated the stories that Charlotte told Wilbur? _____ (Chapter 14)

    A. Fern's mother found them fascinating.

    B. Fern's mother thought Fern was making them up.

    C. Fern's mother thought Fern was telling the stories just as she actually heard them.

19. What was the "duty" of the crickets? _____ (Chapter 15)

    A. to warn everyone of a heat wave

    B. to warn everyone that summer was over

    C. to warn everyone that winter was over

20. When Charlotte wrote RADIANT in her web, Wilbur tried to do this. _____ (Chapter 15)

    A. smile

    B. stand still

    C. glow

21. Wilbur looked forward to the county fair. He thought that if he won some prize money, Mr. Zuckerman would do this. _____ (Chapter 15)

    A. let him have more food

    B. let him have some pig friends

    C. let him live

22. Charlotte said she might not be able to accompany Wilbur to the fair, and she told him this. _____ (Chapter 15)

    A. She said it was almost time for her to make an egg sac.

    B. She said she was too small, and might get lost at a big fair.

    C. She said she was afraid Avery might see her and kill her.

23. What did Templeton think about boys when Avery crawled on all fours pretending to be a pig? _____ (Chapter 16)

    A. Templeton thought boys were fantastic creatures.

    B. Templeton thought boys were lovable creatures.

    C. Templeton thought boys were intelligent creatures.

24. The first sign of coming spring in the barn cellar was hearing the chorus of these animals? _____ (Chapter 22)

    A. sheep

    B. spiders

    C. frogs

25. Charlotte's Web had a happy ending, in spite of Charlotte's death. How did Wilbur live out the rest of his life? _____ (Chapter 22)

    A. He was never killed by the farmers.

    B. He always enjoyed the company of Charlotte's children and grandchildren.

    C. Both A and B

You can find the answers to these questions on page 89.

42

LITERATURE GUIDE FOUR

I Survived the Sinking

of the Titanic, 1912

I Survived Series

By Lauren Tarshis

Chapter Questions

Student Instructions: Read the book and answer the questions as you finish each chapter. If you need help, you may look in the book for help.

1. Who is the main character in this story? _____ (Chapter 1)

    A. Papa

    B. Mama

    C. George

2. The first chapter started with the sinking of the Titanic. The second chapter goes back in time, called a flashback. It went back in time to _____ (Chapter 2)

    A. a week earlier

    B. 19 hours earlier

    C. one year earlier

3. George and his sister Phoebe were invited to go on a trip on the Titanic with this person. _____ (Chapter3)

    A. their uncle

    B. Aunt Daisy

    C. Enzo

4. George met the builder of the Titanic, who said that no ship was safer. His name was _____ (Chapter 4)

    A. Mr. Andrews

    B. Mr. Marco

    C. Mr. James

5. In chapter five, George gets an idea to see something in a wooden crate on the ship. He wanted to see this. _____ (Chapter 5)

    A. an Egyptian mummy

    B. a small model of the ship

    C. a map of the world

6. Chapter six has another flashback. George remembered last October, when he was in the woods and encountered this. _____ (Chapter 6)

   A. a black bear

   B. a black panther

   C. a black German Shepherd

7. George sneaked down to the hold where crates and trunks were stored. The scar faced man was about to lift the lid off a crate, when this happened. _____ (Chapter 7)

   A. A bright light shown in his face.

   B. Aunt Daisy caught him and scolded him.

   C. There was a tremendous noise and the ship started shaking.

8. An eerie silence surrounded George and he realized this. _____ (Chapter 8)

   A. Everyone was quietly sleeping.

   B. A gentle snow was falling.

   C. The engines had been turned off.

9. In chapter nine, who was missing? _____ (Chapter 9)

   A. George

   B. Aunt Daisy

   C. George's sister Phoebe

10. In chapter ten, they came to this realization. _____ (Chapter 10)

   A. The Titanic was filling with water from the sea.

   B. The Titanic was unsinkable.

   C. The Titanic hit an island.

11. The entire ship catapulted forward. People fell _____ (Chapter 11)

    A. but got up easily.

    B. but continued to think it was just a drill.

    C. and were toppling like dominoes.

12. George helped people move to safety when he remembered this. _____
    (Chapter 12)

    A. He remembered where the baggage department was.

    B. He remembered where the ladders were.

    C. He remembered where the engines were.

13. George and Marco were saved because of this. _____ (Chapter 13)

    A. They got in a lifeboat.

    B. A helicopter rescued them.

    C. They stayed on the Titanic until someone came to get them.

14. After drifting in the lifeboat, they were rescued by _____ (Chapter 14)

    A. a ship called the Titanic II.

    B. a ship called the Carpathia.

    C. a ship called the Tarshis.

15. George thought there was a mummy princess on the Titanic that caused bad
    luck, but he found out the princess was only this. _____ (Chapter 15)

    A. a dog

    B. a cat

    C. a panther

16. Once George was safely back home with Papa on the farm, he and Papa decided to build _____ (Chapter 16)

    A. Titanic II

    B. a nice little boat for their pond

    C. a canoe for the river

(The next 4 questions are from the pages at the back of the book called *Facts about the Titanic*.)

17. How much did the Titanic weigh? _____ (Facts pages)

    A. 50,000 pounds

    B. 50,000 tons

18. How many people were on the Titanic? _____ (Facts pages)

    A. 1229

    B. 2229

19. How many countries did the passengers come from? _____ (Facts pages)

    A. 18

    B. 28

20. Most of the crew came from these two countries. _____ (Facts pages)

    A. England and Ireland

    B. England and China

    C. Ireland and South America

Student, when you've checked and corrected all your answers in this literature guide and you've read every page in the book, then take the End of the Book Test.

You can find the answers to these questions on page 90.

I Survived the Sinking

of the Titanic, 1912

I Survived Series

By Lauren Tarshis

End of the Book Test

<u>Student Instructions</u>: Student, each question is worth 4 points. Let's see how well you've read this exciting book. You may use this as an open book test and complete it within a 30-minute time limit. After you take the test, have your teacher/parent score the test for you. Then correct the wrong answers by reviewing the book for the correct answers.

1. What point of view is this written in? _____ (Chapter 1)

   A. first person - I, my, me

   B. second person - you, your

   C. third person - he/she, his/hers, him/her

2. How old was the main character, George Calder? _____ (Chapter 1)

   A. 8

   B. 10

   C. 12

3. George sometimes got into trouble. He didn't mean to, but he did this. _____
   (Chapter 3)

   A. He just got these great ideas.

   B. His sister made him get into trouble.

   C. He liked to annoy his Aunt Daisy.

4. George was very interested in the ship. The builder, Mr. Andrews, made this
   prediction about George. _____ (Chapter 4)

   A. George would one day build a ship of his own.

   B. George would one day be a baseball player.

   C. George would one day build a skyscraper.

5. Mr. Stead said nothing could harm the Titanic. Not even this. _____ (Chapter 5)

   A. bad weather

   B. a lot of baggage

   C. the curse of a mummy

6. George thought Henry had eyes in the back of his head. What did he mean? _____ (Chapter 6)

    A. Henry was a monster.

    B. Henry walked backwards.

    C. Henry always seemed to see him wherever he went.

7. A simile compares two different things with the word *like* or *as*. This simile is on page 28. Thinking about Mama was like standing close to a fire. What did that mean? _____ (Chapter 6)

    A. warm at first, but hurtful if you get too close

    B. warm at first, but then cool

    C. warm at first, but then the fire goes out

8. What actions showed George was happy? _____ (Chapter 7)

    A. He whistled a tune.

    B. He practically skipped along the hallway.

    C. He laughed loudly.

9. What was the purpose of leaving a trail of crumbs or lemon drops? _____ (Chapter 7)

    A. You could have a snack.

    B. You could follow the trail if someone got lost.

    C. You could play pick-up-quick.

10. At first, people on the Titanic did not realize they were in trouble. They were standing on the deck laughing. What were they laughing at? _____ (Chapter 8)

    A. Some young men were throwing ice at each other like kids having a snowball fight.

    B. Some clowns were performing on deck.

    C. Some singers were singing funny songs.

11. What time was it when Aunt Daisy and the kids were told to go up on deck because the ship hit an iceberg? _____ (Chapter 9)

    A. twelve noon

    B. 9:00 in the evening

    C. after midnight

12. What was their first reaction to having to wear life jackets and get on deck? _____ (Chapter 10)

    A. They thought they would drown.

    B. They thought they reached an island.

    C. They thought it would be a big joke to laugh at over breakfast in the morning.

13. Enzo kept saying, "See! See!" Then George realized he meant this. _____ (Chapter 10)

    A. He was trying to tell them the sea water was coming into the Titanic.

    B. He wanted George to see Marco.

    C. He wanted George to play hide and seek with him.

14. Having a foghorn voice meant this. _____ (Chapter 11)

    A. The voice could only make sounds and not say words.

    B. The voice was loud like a foghorn.

    C. The voice was used when the foghorn was broken.

15. An officer on the ship spoke to Marco. "Women and children only, sir," he said somberly. What does somberly mean? _____ (Chapter 12)

    A. seriously, sadly

    B. angrily

    C. quickly

16. George wasn't allowed to get on the lifeboat. The officer said this. _____
(Chapter 12)

    A. Get in the next boat.

    B. Wait your turn.

    C. No more room.

17. At the end of chapter twelve, George fell, smashing his head on the deck. And then there was silence. Why was there silence? _____ (Chapter 12)

    A. He was unconscious.

    B. The music stopped.

    C. Everyone got quiet.

18. "It's time to go," Marco said. Where did they have to go? _____ (Chapter 13)

    A. back to their rooms

    B. into the water

    C. into a lifeboat

19. A simile compares two things. What does the simile on page 74 compare the cold water to? _____ (Chapter 13)

    A. ice crystals stabbing him

    B. millions of needles stabbing him

    C. sharp knives stabbing him

20. George grabbed the side of a small canvas boat, but someone pushed his hand off. Why? _____ (Chapter 13)

    A. The man thought George was a convict.

    B. The man thought George would put them all in the water.

    C. The man thought George could swim safely.

21. Who helped George when he was trying to get Marco into the boat? _____
(Chapter 13)

    A. Aunt Daisy

    B. Phoebe

    C. the scar-faced man

22. How many people made it out of the water? _____ (Chapter 15)

    A. 600

    B. 700

    C. 800

(The next three questions are from the pages "Facts about the Titanic.")

23. How was the size of the Titanic described? _____

    A. four city blocks long

    B. five city blocks long

    C. six city blocks long

24. How many dogs survived the Titanic? _____

    A. 9

    B. 2

    C. 3

25. The Titanic sank to the bottom of the ocean and was not discovered until this year. _____

    A. 1985

    B. 1975

    C. 1995

You can find the answers to these questions on page 91.

LITERATURE GUIDE FIVE

The Knight at Dawn

Magic Tree House #2

By Mary Pope Osborne

Chapter Questions

Student Instructions: Read the book and answer the questions as you finish each chapter. If you need help, you may look in the book for help.

1. Jack and Annie prepared to go to the magic tree house, and Annie took a magic wand with her. What did Annie call a magic wand? _____ (Chapter 1)

   A. a stick from the tree

   B. a flashlight

   C. a pencil

2. Jack and Annie were able to go back in time when they did this. _____ (Chapter 2)

   A. pointed to a picture in a book

   B. waved a magic wand

   C. wished upon a star

3. When Jack and Annie went back in time, they saw a castle and a drawbridge. The drawbridge was over this. _____ (Chapter 3)

   A. a river

   B. a moat with crocodiles in it

   C. a gently flowing stream

4. Jack and Annie went into the castle and saw this. _____ (Chapter 4)

   A. a king and queen sitting on thrones

   B. large empty rooms

   C. a Great Hall where there was a large feast

5. Jack found this out when he tried on a helmet. _____ (Chapter 5)

   A. It was made of plastic.

   B. It was so heavy he could not lift his head.

   C. It was lightweight.

6. Jack and Annie were thrown into a miserable dungeon, but were able to escape when Annie did this. _____ (Chapter 6)

   A. She screamed at the top of her lungs.

   B. She fainted dead away.

   C. She shined her flashlight at the guards, and it scared them.

7. They found a secret tunnel that lead to this. _____ (Chapter 7)

    A.   the moat

    B.   the Great Room

    C.   the drawbridge

8. They were trapped in the still, cold darkness when they heard and saw this. _____ (Chapter 8)

    A. a knight on a horse

    B. a crocodile with sharp teeth

    C. their parents

9. Who rescued them? _____ (Chapter 9)

    A. their parents

    B. a king and queen

    C. a knight

10. They made it safely back home, and Jack noticed the same letter on the ancient bookmark. He knew the mystery of who owned all the books in the tree house started with this letter. _____ (Chapter 10)

    A. J

    B. A

    C. M

Student, when you've checked and corrected all your answers in this literature guide and you've read every page in the book, then take the End of the Book Test.

You can find the answers to these questions on page 92.

The Knight at Dawn

Magic Tree House #2

By Mary Pope Osborne

End of the Book Test

<u>Student Instructions</u>: Student, each question is worth 4 points. Let's see how well you've read this exciting book. You may use this as an open book test and complete it within a 30-minute time limit. After you take the test, have your teacher/parent score the test for you. Then correct the wrong answers by reviewing the book for the correct answers.

1. Jack thought so many strange things happened yesterday. One strange thing that happened was this. _____ (Chapter 1)

   A. He overslept.

   B. He went back to the time of dinosaurs.

   C. He talked to his third grade teacher.

2. It was almost dawn. What does dawn mean? _____ (Chapter 1)

   A. sunrise

   B. sunset

   C. noon

3. Why did Jack and Annie want the dog to be quiet? _____ (Chapter 1)

   A. They didn't like dogs.

   B. They already fed the dog.

   C. They didn't want the dog to wake up their parents.

4. How had Jack seen a real live Tyrannosaurus Rex? _____ (Chapter 2)

   A. A book in the magic tree house took them back to the time of dinosaurs.

   B. He saw one in a museum.

   C. He saw one on a website.

5. What does whinny mean? _____ (Chapter 2)

   A. the sound a cat makes

   B. the sound a squirrel makes

   C. the sound a horse makes

6. What were hawks trained to do? _____ (Chapter 3)

   A. hunt other birds and mice

   B. talk like parrots

   C. perform tricks with the king's magician

7. What are fanfares? _____ (Chapter 3)

   A. drums and horns played to announce dishes in a large feast

   B. fans to cool the guests

   C. jugglers performing for the king and queen

8. Annie vanished through a gate. What does vanished mean? _____ (Chapter 3)

   A. dashed

   B. disappeared

   C. departed

9. "Halt!" someone shouted. What does halt mean? _____ (Chapter 4)

   A. stop

   B. go away

   C. come here

10. What are some examples of armory? _____ (Chapter 5)

    A. leg plates, breastplates, and helmets

    B. torches and flashlights

    C. castles and moats

11. Jack's helmet was yanked off. What does yanked mean? _____ (Chapter 5)

    A. slid off slowly

    B. pulled off roughly

    C. lifted off gently

12. What did the dungeon look like? _____ (Chapter 6)

    A. a comfortable lounge

    B. a filthy place with puddles and chains

    C. a rich, elegant castle room

13. His hands were trembling as he flipped through the pages of the castle book. Why was Jack trembling? _____ (Chapter 7)

    A. He was scared.

    B. He was excited.

    C. He was joyful.

14. How did Jack and Annie escape? _____ (Chapter 7)

    A. through the roof

    B. through a trapdoor

    C. up a ladder

15. The light got dimmer and dimmer. What does dimmer mean? _____ (Chapter 7)

    A. brighter

    B. duller

    C. sharper

16. When Jack fell into the moat, he felt a live wet thing. What was it? _____ (Chapter 8)

    A. a crocodile

    B. a knight

    C. Annie

17. The knight dismounted. What does dismounted mean? _____ (Chapter 9)

    A. got off

    B. got on

    C. got away from

18. How did Jack feel when he was on the back of the knight's horse? _____
    (Chapter 9)

    A. scared and small

    B. brave and very powerful

    C. wet and tired

19. When Jack and Annie saw the ladder to the tree house, the knight helped
    them off the horse. What did Jack and Annie do then? _____ (Chapter 9)

    A. They bowed to the knight.

    B. They shook his hand.

    C. They gave him a high five.

20. After Jack and Annie got off the knight's horse, what did the knight do?
    _____ (Chapter 9)

    A. He decided to walk instead of riding his horse.

    B. He wanted to go with Jack and Annie.

    C. He got back on his horse and rode off through the mist.

21. Why were they looking for the Pennsylvania book? _____ (Chapter 9)

    A. They wanted to go home to Pennsylvania.

    B. They wanted to learn more about Pennsylvania.

    C. They wanted to see if knights lived in Pennsylvania.

22. Annie was scooting out of the tree house. What does scooting mean?
    _____ (Chapter 10)

    A. moving quickly

    B. moving slowly

    C. marching

23. When they got back home this happened. _____ (Chapter 10)

    A. Their parents were waiting for them on the front porch.

    B. Their parents called the police to file a missing person report.

    C. Their parents didn't realize they were gone.

24. The bookmark seemed ancient. What does ancient mean? _____ (Chapter 10)

    A. very old

    B. very messy

    C. very new

25. The letter on the bookmark was the same as the letter on this. _____
(Chapter 10)

    A. the knight's helmet

    B. the gold medallion

    C. the door of the castle

You can find the answers to these questions on page 93.

LITERATURE GUIDE SIX

I Survived the Battle

of Gettysburg, 1863

I Survived Series

By Lauren Tarshis

Chapter Questions

Student Instructions: Read the book and answer the questions as you finish each chapter. If you need help, you may look in the book for help.

1. This story is about an eleven-year-old boy named Thomas and his five-year-old sister Birdie. The story begins with Thomas and northern soldiers on a battlefield in Pennsylvania. Why were the northern soldiers fighting in this battle? _____ (Chapter 1)

   A. to gain more land

   B. to free slaves

   C. to fight against England

2. Chapter two is a flashback going back in time before the Battle of Gettysburg. What was the time? _____ (Chapter 2)

   A. 3 weeks earlier

   B. 3 months earlier

   C. 3 weeks earlier

3. Thomas carried Birdie and ran through the woods to escape from _____ (Chapter 3)

   A. slave catchers

   B. his cousin

   C. a wolf

4. Birdie started to whimper because she saw a _____ (Chapter 4)

   A. bobcat

   B. skunk

   C. hawk

5. How did the skunk actually help Thomas and Birdie? _____ (Chapter 5)

   A. The soldiers ran into the woods away from the skunk.

   B. The soldiers shot the skunk.

   C. The soldiers ignored the skunk.

71

6. The story of Thomas and the skunk had swept through the soldiers' camp because _____ (Chapter 6)

   A. they liked skunks.

   B. they had thrown the skunk at their enemy.

   C. they were squirted by the skunk.

7. Why were Thomas and Birdie feeling safe with the soldiers in blue uniforms? _____ (Chapter 7)

   A. The soldiers in blue were from the South.

   B. The soldiers in blue were fighting to free the slaves.

   C. The soldiers in blue wanted to kill Thomas and Birdie, but the children didn't know it.

8. How many soldiers were killed or wounded in Fredericksburg? _____ (Chapter 8)

   A. 1,200

   B. 12,000

   C. 120,000

9. Henry made this promise to Thomas and Birdie. _____ (Chapter 9)

   A. They would go to school and learn to read.

   B. They would go back to Virginia when the war was over.

   C. They would go to New York City.

10. What was on Birdie's doll? _____ (Chapter 10)

   A. a bird

   B. blood

   C. a skunk

11. For how much money did the soldiers think they could sell Thomas? _____
    (Chapter 11)

    A. ten dollars

    B. a hundred dollars

    C. a thousand dollars

12. Thomas and Birdie had been captured, but they were rescued by _____
    (Chapter 12)
    A. Confederate soldiers

    B. Union soldiers

13. Thomas and Birdie saw some black men. Who were they? _____ (Chapter 13)

    A. slaves

    B. freed slaves

14. What happened at the end of chapter fourteen? _____ (Chapter 14)

    A. Thomas got shot.

    B. Birdie got shot.

    C. Henry got shot.

15. Who was calling Thomas's name? _____ (Chapter 15)

    A. Captain Campbell

    B. Henry

    C. Clem

16. Chapter sixteen moves ahead in time to November, five months after the
    Battle of Gettysburg. Now Thomas and Birdie were going to school in
    Vermont. What was unusual about this? _____ (Chapter 16)

    A. Thomas was never allowed to go to school when he was a slave at Knox
       Farm.

    B. Thomas never wanted to go to school, but now he was forced to go.

Student, when you've checked and corrected all your answers in this literature guide and you've read every page in the book, then take the End of the Book Test.

You can find the answers to these questions on page 94.

I Survived the Battle of Gettysburg, 1863

I Survived Series

By Lauren Tarshis

End of the Book Test

<u>Student Instructions:</u> Student, each question is worth 4 points. Let's see how well you've read this exciting book. You may use this as an open book test and complete it within a 30-minute time limit. After you take the test, have your teacher/parent score the test for you. Then correct the wrong answers by reviewing the book for the correct answers.

1. Which side of the Civil War was fighting to end slavery? _____ (Chapter 1)

   A. North

   B. South

2. What was the difference between the North and the South? _____ (Chapter 2)

   A. Slavery was illegal in the North.

   B. Slavery was legal in the North.

3. What would happen to runaway slaves if they were caught by anyone fighting for the South? _____ (Chapter 3)

   A. They'd be set free.

   B. They'd be whipped or worse.

   C. They'd be rewarded.

4. What was a Yankee? _____ (Chapter 4)

   A. a soldier fighting for the North

   B. a soldier fighting for the South

5. What was a Rebel? _____ (Chapter 5)

   A. a soldier fighting for the North

   B. a soldier fighting for the South

6. What is a bugler? _____ (Chapter 6)

   A. someone who plays a bugle, a horn

   B. someone who rides a horse

   C. someone who shoots a cannon

7. How did the Rebel soldiers scare the Union soldiers? _____ (Chapter 7)

   A. with a stampede of horses

   B. with a ferocious battle cry

C. with the sound of a cannon

8. Which side won the battle of Fredericksburg? _____ (Chapter 8)

   A. South

   B. North

9. Why hadn't Thomas learned how to read or write? _____ (Chapter 9)

   A. It was illegal for slaves to learn to read and write.

   B. Thomas had no interest in learning to read or write.

10. What was a musket? _____ (Chapter 10)

   A. gunpowder

   B. a gun, rifle

   C. a sword

11. Who were the Rebel cavalry kidnapping? _____ (Chapter 11)

   A. British soldiers

   B. escaped slaves

12. When people bought slaves, what did they check? _____ (Chapter 12)

   A. their animals

   B. their credentials

   C. their teeth

13. What news was given about the fighting at Gettysburg on July 2nd? _____
    (Chapter 13)
    A. The Rebel troops had been outnumbered.

   B. The Union troops had been outnumbered.

14. In chapter fourteen, we read that the soldiers were waving gleaming swords.
In this sentence, what does gleaming mean? _____ (Chapter 14)

   A. smiling

   B. shining

C. shivering

15. We read that Thomas felt that the world spun around him, the sky fell, and the air turned bright white? Why did Thomas feel that? _____ (Chapter 14)

A. He was up so high.

B. He had been shot by a bullet.

C. He saw snow in the sky.

16. How had a book saved Thomas's life? _____ (Chapter 15)

A. It was a very long book.

B. It was a magic book.

C. It was a tin-covered book.

(The rest of the questions are taken from the grey pages.)

17. How many years did the Civil War last? _____

A. 4

B. 5

C. 6

18. How many people died in the Civil War? _____

A. 7,500

B. 75,000

C. 750,000

19. By 1860 how many slaves were there? _____

A. 4000

B. 400,000

C. 4,000,000

20. The author writes that her nineteen and twenty-two-year-old sons would have been soldiers in the Civil War if they lived at that time in history. Why? _____

    A. All young men at that time were soldiers.

    B. They liked shooting people.

21. The Gettysburg Address was a speech given by President Abraham Lincoln. How long did that famous speech last? _____

    A. 2 minutes

    B. 12 minutes

    C. 20 minutes

22. The first sentence of the Gettysburg Address says our nation was dedicated to the proposition that _____

    A. all men must work

    B. all men are created equal

23. Lincoln wrote this in his Gettysburg Address speech. "Four score and seven years ago our fathers brought forth on this continent a new nation conceived in liberty…." If a score is equal to 20 years, how long ago was four score and seven? _____

    A. 67

    B. 77

    C. 87

24. What did Lincoln think about what he said in his speech? _____

    A. It would long be remembered.

    B. It would not long be remembered.

25. What did Lincoln say in his speech about those who died in the war? _____

    A. They have died in vain.

    B. They shall not have died in vain.

You can find the answers to these questions on page 95.

Student, this now completes your six-book set. Congratulations!

Look for more exciting adventures with literature guides

From Carolyn Oravitz.

Answer Sheets

MR. POPPER' S PENGUINS
BY RICHARD AND FLORENCE ATWATER

CHAPTER QUESTIONS

1.	C	11.	A
2.	B	12.	C
3.	A	13.	A
4.	C	14.	A
5.	B	15.	C
6.	B	16.	B
7.	C	17.	C
8.	C	18.	C
9.	A	19.	A
10.	A	20.	B

MR. POPPER'S PENGUINS
BY RICHARD AND FLORENCE ATWATER

END OF THE BOOK TEST

1. C
2. A
3. B
4. C
5. B
6. A
7. C
8. B
9. C
10. B
11. B
12. C
13. C

14. B
15. A
16. A
17. A
18. C
19. A
20. A
21. B
22. C
23. C
24. A
25. B

STOLEN! A PONY CALLED PEBBLES
BY WENDY ORR

CHAPTER QUESTIONS

1. A
2. B
3. C
4. A
5. B
6. C
7. A
8. B
9. C
10. B
11. C

STOLEN! A PONY CALLED PEBBLES
BY WENDY ORR

END OF THE BOOK TEST

1.	A	14.	B
2.	C	15.	C
3.	B	16.	C
4.	C	17.	B
5.	B	18.	A
6.	A	19.	B
7.	C	20.	A
8.	A	21.	C
9.	A	22.	A
10.	A	23.	B
11.	B	24.	C
12.	B	25.	B
13.	B		

CHARLOTTE'S WEB
BY E. B. WHITE

CHAPTER QUESTIONS

1.	C	12.	C
2.	A	13.	B
3.	C	14.	C
4.	B	15.	B
5.	A	16.	B
6.	A	17.	C
7.	A	18.	A
8.	A	19.	C
9.	A	20.	A
10.	B	21.	B
11.	B	22.	B

CHARLOTTE'S WEB
BY E. B. WHITE

END OF THE BOOK TEST

1. B
2. A
3. A
4. C
5. B
6. B
7. A
8. A
9. C
10. C
11. C
12. A
13. B

14. A
15. B
16. C
17. A
18. B
19. B
20. C
21. C
22. A
23. A
24. C
25. C

I SURVIVED THE SINKING OF THE TITANIC, 1912

I SURVIVED SERIES
BY LAUREN TARSHIS

CHAPTER QUESTIONS

1.	C	11.	C
2.	B	12.	B
3.	B	13.	A
4.	A	14.	B
5.	A	15.	B
6.	B	16.	B
7.	C	17.	B
8.	C	18.	B
9.	C	19.	B
10.	A	20.	A

I SURVIVED THE SINKING OF THE TITANIC, 1912

I SURVIVED SERIES
BY LAUREN TARSHIS

END OF THE BOOK TEST

1. C
2. B
3. A
4. A
5. C
6. C
7. A
8. B
9. B
10. A
11. C
12. C
13. A

14. B
15. A
16. C
17. A
18. B
19. B
20. B
21. C
22. B
23. A
24. C
25. A

THE KNIGHT AT DAWN
MAGIC TREE HOUSE #2
BY MARY POPE OSBORNE

CHAPTER QUESTIONS

1. B
2. A
3. B
4. C
5. B
6. C
7. A
8. A
9. C
10. C

THE KNIGHT AT DAWN

MAGIC TREE HOUSE #2
BY MARY POPE OSBORNE

END OF THE BOOK TEST

1.	B	14.	B
2.	A	15.	B
3.	C	16.	C
4.	A	17.	A
5.	C	18.	B
6.	A	19.	A
7.	A	20.	C
8.	B	21.	A
9.	A	22.	A
10.	A	23.	C
11.	B	24.	A
12.	B	25.	B
13.	A		

I SURVIVED THE BATTLE OF GETTYSBURG, 1863
I SURVIVED SERIES
BY LAUREN TARSHIS

CHAPTER QUESTIONS

1. B
2. A
3. A
4. B
5. A
6. B
7. B
8. B

9. A
10. B
11. C
12. B
13. B
14. A
15. C
16. A

I SURVIVED THE BATTLE OF GETTYSBURG, 1863
I SURVIVED SERIES
BY LAUREN TARSHIS

END OF THE BOOK TEST

1. A
2. A
3. B
4. A
5. B
6. A
7. B
8. A
9. A
10. B
11. B
12. C
13. B

14. B
15. B
16. C
17. A
18. C
19. C
20. A
21. A
22. B
23. C
24. B
25. B

ABOUT THE AUTHOR

Author Carolyn Oravitz - *With 30 years of teaching experience and certificates in both elementary education and high school English, author Carolyn Oravitz brings a wealth of experience in teaching reading. Her literature guides are designed to motivate children to develop a love for reading while developing the necessary reading comprehension and vocabulary skills to succeed.*